D1549488

Ref

British Lorries 1945~1975

British Lorries
1945~1975

S. W. Stevens-Stratten, FRSA.

LONDON
IAN ALLAN LTD

First published 1978

ISBN 0 7110 0736 5

© Ian Allan Ltd, 1978

Published by Ian Allan Ltd, Shepperton, Surrey,
and printed in the United Kingdom by
Ian Allan Printing Ltd

Contents

Introduction

Road transport has changed considerably in the 30year period covered by this book. The startline, 1945, the end of the Second World War, saw the roads of Great Britain starved of new vehicles of all types, and transport operators were forced to continue using lorries and vans that would normally have been replaced. It was a tribute to British engineering that many of them continued to give good service, although already past their prime. With the return to peacetime the motor vehicle manufacturers were once again able to turn to their normal production, but to meet demand they continued to produce the same type of vehicle as they had done in 1939. Many of these designs are featured in the companion book *British Lorries 1900-1945* by my colleague Charles F. Klapper.

It was not long, however, before new designs began to appear. Many improvements were incorporated in the new vehicles, some of these as a result of wartime experiences and developments in other forms of transport. Vehicles became larger, more powerful and more refined, but the technical development also kept apace of the times — as did provision for drivers' comfort.

During the 30 years many famous vehicle manufacturers have disappeared or lost their autonomy. Several have been swallowed up in the British Leyland empire; some kept their name, but their products are indistinquishable from others in allied stables.

Nationalisation of the road haulage industry in 1947 saw the end of many interesting operators and of some distinctive liveries. Fortunately these losses were compensated by the many well-known companies in the manufacturing and distributive trades operating their own fleet of vehicles. Road transport undoubtedly benefited by the cut-backs of British Rail and the curtailing of many railway lines under the regime of Dr Beeching. The lorry is now supreme for the transport of goods from door to door and with the advent of the motorway network — which is still being extended — large loads can travel to their destination far more quickly and without any need for transhipment en route.

The range of operation has been extended beyond the shores of the British Isles with the facilities offered by the 'roll-on, roll-off' ferries plying between this country and the Continent. This has led to much inter-change of traffic and the number of foreign registered vehicles on our roads has increased rapidly; it will probably rise further as the European Economic Community — The 'Common Market' — becomes stronger.

The popular press, radio and television refer to these Continental vehicles and in fact all large vehicles — as 'Juggernauts', a term which the author feels is not only inapt but unjust. The dictionary states that a Juggernaut was a chariot taken in procession when thousands contended for the honour of dragging the vehicle and many devotees threw themselves under its wheels to be crushed! It can also refer to a relentless inhuman force which destroys blindly anything that comes in its way. That is hardly fair comment on the drivers or operators of heavy goods vehicles which are so needed for our economy and must surely benefit our standard of living.

The lifting of many legal restrictions have certainly had an effect on the size and speed of lorries and vans, but at the same time there is now no need to manufacture a very lightweight vehicle to carry over three tons at a speed of 30mph. Much attention has been given to the quietening of engines and the emission of fumes and polution. Drivers' comfort has been particularly catered for, and the driving of his vehicle and its heavy load has been made easier; cab ventilation, heating, adjustable seats, automatic transmission, power assisted steering — all make for greater safety. There is also legislation to ensure that the driver cannot drive more than a certain number of hours, unlike the old days when drivers were at the wheel for nearly 24hr without a break.

The prime mover, or tractive unit, with a high-capacity semi-trailer has found favour with many operators. Its advantage is that at each end of the run one trailer can be unloading or loading, while a third is on the road between the two points, and all need only the one power unit to operate economically.

The flamboyant designs of the early post-war period have gone. Standardisation has become more obvious and there is less specialised bodywork, but in both cases more practical vehicles have evolved. In spite of this there is, generally speaking, an even greater interest in road transport than ever before. I trust it will continue and that the illustrations in this book will bring back memories and be of interest.

In compiling this book I have tried not to

duplicate the earlier book *British Lorries 1900-1945,* although obviously some overlapping is bound to occur, particularly in the short introductory notes to each chapter. This is not meant to be a complete history of the manufacturer, for it tries to keep within the title of this volume, which is the period 1945-75. The illustrations are in no sense to be regarded as showing all the models produced by the makers in the past 30 years, but merely an interesting selection chosen to depict some of the progress made, with the emphasis on vehicles which could be seen on the roads in the 1960s.

While I would not be so presumptuous as to forecast the future, I do not think that the next 30 years will see as many changes as the previous period, unless it is in the type of fuel, or economies that may be made in its use.

All photographs used in this volume are from the Ian Allan Library or my own collection.

S. W. Stevens-Stratten
Epsom   1976

Below: Cab interior of ERF European Tractive Unit.

AEC

The history of the Associated Equipment Company goes back to 1906, the days of the Vanguard buses, one of the many independent London operators who joined to form the London General Omnibus Co. Later AEC became a separate company in 1912 and produced the immortal B type bus. A lorry on this chassis followed, then the Y type, and by the mid-1920s several commercial vehicle chassis were available. In the 1930s AEC — builders of London's Buses — were among the largest commercial vehicle manufacturers in the United Kingdom.

During the Second World War the production of AEC vehicles and equipment was impressive: 9,620 Matador 4 × 4 medium artillery tractors; 1,514 Marshall six-wheel 2,500gal refuelling tankers for the RAF; 192 Marshall six-wheel vehicles for Coles cranes; 185 Marshall six-wheel vehicles for mobile oxygen plants; 629 armoured cars; and oil engines for Valentine tanks and many other items that were vital to the Services and the country generally.

With the cessation of hostilities, AEC once more turned their attention to the civilian markets and their first designs were little changed from the models they manufactured before the war. In 1948 the range consisted of: the Matador and Monarch, both four-wheel vehicles of 12tons gross weight, the former capable

of hauling a trailer; the Mammoth Major six-wheeler of 19tons gross weight; and the Mammoth Major eight- wheeler of 22tons gross weight.

In 1948 AEC Ltd took over control of the old-established firms of Maudslay Motor Co Ltd of Alcester (near Coventry) and Crossley Motors. Shortly after this the parent company changed its name to Associated Commercial Vehicles Ltd, but the historic and well-known initials AEC were kept for the production and design of their products. A year later the bodybuilding firm of Park Royal Vehicles Ltd and its subsidiary Charles H. Roe Ltd of Leeds were acquired by the Group, but as their main production was passenger vehicle bodies it had little effect on the commerical vehicle scene.

In 1953 the Mercury chassis was introduced to the range. Its payload of 8tons could be carried at a cruising speed of 40mph. It proved popular, and a year later a redesigned cab was introduced on all models.

The firm decided to enter the earth-moving field in 1957 and introduced a large six-wheeled 10cu yd 'Dumptruk', later building several sizes, including an 18cu yd four-axle model. Production of 'Dumptruks' ceased after a period of approximately ten years.

Another acquisition was made in 1961 when Transport Equipment (Thornycroft) Ltd of Basingstoke was absorbed into the ACV empire and the production of Thornycroft vehicles ceased, except for some specialised models such as the Antar tractor and some airport fire-fighting models.

August 1962 saw Associated Commercial Vehicles merged with Leyland Motors. Although some years elapsed before any outward changes were noticed, production has now been rationalised.

In 1968 a new Mammoth Major was produced with a V8 oil engine developing 247bhp and this was followed by a Marshall lightweight eight-wheeler. Both vehicles were fitted with the Ergomatic cab, which had appeared some time earlier and was common to vehicles of the Leyland badge.

In 1970 the AEC production consisted of Mercury, Monarch and Mandator two-axle vehicles; Marshall and Mammoth Major 6, three-axle types and the Marshall 8 × 4 and Mammoth Major 8 four-axle types.

Below: Mammoth Major eight-wheeler, a design which had continued since 1933 with little outward change.

Top: A Monarch tipper operated by BRS. This chassis was available with three wheelbases — 14ft 7in, 16 ft 7in or the short 12ft 1in version as shown here. An AEC six-cylinder 7.7litre diesel engine was fitted.

Above: This Mammoth Major chassis carries a Thompson-built 3,000gal stainless steel tank. It is one of a fleet used by the operator to carry milk over long distances.

Above: Built to the maximum dimensions permitted in 1956, this Mammoth Major has an overall length of 30ft and is 7ft 8in wide. It was the first 24ton gvw chassis to enter the service of Shell-Mex & BP Ltd, carrying 4,000gal of fuel in five separate compartments. The vehicle has a five-speed gearbox and power-assisted steering.

Centre left: A short-wheelbase Mercury tractor with an Eagle 12-14ton low-loading semi-trailer operated by Dallas of New Malden, Surrey. This improved type cab and radiator was introduced on the new Mercury range when it made its appearance in 1954 and subsequently was used on all other vehicles in the AEC range.

Bottom left: The old order changes in 1962 as Shell-Mex & BP Ltd dropped their livery of red and green in favour of yellow and grey. This 3,700gal articulated unit has a two-compartment tank with air discharge at 35lb per sq in. The prime mover is a Mandator tractor fitted with six-speed overdrive gearbox and a double-reduction rear axle.

11

Above: From the mid-1960s AEC vehicles were equipped with the new Ergomatic cab as shown in this illustration of a Mammoth Major 30ton gvw tipper. It is fitted with the AV760 fuel injection six-cylinder diesel engine with a cubic capacity of 12.47litre.

Right: The interior of a cab on a modern Mandator tractor. It has a flat floor, comfortable double crew seats, provision for heating and fresh air flow, and is insulated against noise.

Albion

The Albion Motor Car Co was founded in 1901 in Scotstoun, Glasgow and produced its first commercial vehicle in 1903. It progressed steadily and in the 1930s was a prolific producer of a large range of medium to heavy chassis.

During the war the company produced tank transporters and other military vehicles. Production of civilian types was recommenced in 1947 with a range of six heavy chassis: the CX7 — an eight-wheeler with 14½ tons payload; the CX5 — a six-wheeler for 12 tons payload; the CX1 and CX3 — 7 and 6½ ton four-wheelers; and two lightweight models, the FT3 1 ton and AZ5 1½ tons chassis. All had the well known Albion radiator with the setting sun motif at the top.

In 1951, Albion merged with Leyland and although production continued, it soon became obvious that the Leyland influence was present. This was particularly noticeable in the cab design and from 1968 the old Albion features had virtually disappeared.

The 1970 production programme consisted of two- and three-axle trucks, tippers and tractors in the medium weight range only. The Scotstoun premises have been closed and Albion has lost its identity now, managing the Britsh Leyland factory at Bathgate.

Below: The 1948 6 ton Chieftain (Model FT37A) and the 7½ ton Clydesdale (FT101A) were basically similar and available in four differing wheelbases — 9ft 9in for tippers, 12ft, 14ft and 17ft 6in, the latter in the Chieftain version for pantechnicon bodies. A further alternative was a six-cylinder petrol or a four-cylinder diesel engine for the 6 ton version, the diesel being standard on the 7½ ton vehicle, later also adopted for the smaller model.

Top: This Caledonian eight-wheeled chassis shows the Leyland influence in its cab design. The 4,000gal five-compartment tank body is made by the Steel Barrel Co Ltd and each stainless steel compartment is fitted with steam heated coils.

Above: A Clydesdale tractor with BTC/Charrold semi-trailer capable of carrying 12-15ton of coal for bulk delivery in the Enfield area. Discharge is via a portable conveyor belt which is stored under the body and attached to the rear of the vehicle. The body is 24ft long.

Above: In the 1950s, Albion produced the Claymore for 3ton and 4ton loads. This 'Black Maria' supplied to the Rochdale Police Department is based on the vertical diesel-engined chassis supplied for a 4ton gross load. Petrol-engined models ceased to be manufactured in 1954.

Left: In 1955 a new series of Claymore 3ton and 4ton chassis was introduced, using a new horizontal version of an older diesel power unit which was mounted amidships under the frame. This allowed a cab to be built forward of the front axle, unobstructed by wheel arches. A 10ft or 11ft 10in wheelbase alternative was offered.

15

Above: In 1961 the Chieftain was looking like this version which has a rack for carrying 54 milk churns and a 1,000gal tank. The vehicle is used for collecting milk from farms for delivery to a processing plant.

Below: A Super Reiver 20 six-wheeled tipping lorry in the service of a coal distributor in Bradford. The Ergomatic cab is exactly the same as those fitted to the AEC range of vehicles of similar size.

Atkinson

Above: The largest model built by Atkinson in 1956 was the 15ton eight-wheeler.

Atkinson Lorries Ltd was formed in 1933 to take over the remaining assets and production of the Preston-based firm of that name which had been in existence since 1907 and had originally manufactured steam lorries. Prior to the war four-, six- and eight-wheelers were built, all powered by the well-tried and popular Gardner diesel engine. All models used standardised parts where possible. During the war a few Atkinson vehicles were produced for the civilian market, many of these being fitted with AEC oil engines.

Production recommenced in full in 1948 and continued with unaltered designs until 1953, when the new bow-fronted cab was introduced. To enter the market for the cross-country type of vehicle used by oil-field operators, Atkinson in 1957 introduced the Omega, which was a 6 × 6 vehicle fitted with Rolls-Royce engine.

In the early 1960s Atkinson began manufacturing the Black Knight range of freight vehicles: the Gold Knight chassis for tippers and concrete mixers (with short wheelbase); and the Silver Knight tractive units. The whole 'Knight' range was available as four-, six- or eight-wheelers. During 1968 some Atkinsons were

manufactured with a Krupp (German) cab on a Silver Knight chassis for the European market.

During 1970 Atkinson purchased and acquired the firm of Seddon, who still continued manufacturing their own range. Unusual vehicles were 'The Leader' a rear-steering tractor unit introduced in 1972, and a large 8 × 4 tipping lorry using the Gardner 150 engine, which was also fitted to several trucks. The truck range received names and now consists of the 'Searcher', a 6 × 4 chassis mainly for cement mixers and the 'Defender', an 8 × 4 truck. But the emphasis is on the tractive units for semi-trailers — the 'Venturer' a 6 × 4 unit, and the 'Borderer', a 4 × 2 unit, both offered with Gardner or Cummins engines.

Seddon Motors acquired the control of Atkinson in 1970 becoming Seddon-Atkinson and in 1974 the firm was taken over by International Harvester of America, who already had a European interest when it acquired the Dutch firm of DAF. Production continues without change.

Top: A 7½ton lorry (Model 744) with a drop-sided body for the concrete industry.

Above: In the late 1950s Atkinson introduced a new-look cab to their models although retaining the traditional radiator. This rigid 8 is powered by a Gardner 6LX diesel engine developing 150bhp.

Above: A typical example of the Atkinson prime movers of the 1960s is this T746XA tractor and stainless steel tank semi-trailer. It is painted in the attractive pale blue livery of Monkton Motors Ltd and is on contract hire to a well-known brewery.

Centre left: A Model T7566C 6 × 4 tractor fitted with a Cummins fuel injection 240bhp diesel engine turbo-charged to 400bhp. The wheelbase of the tractor is 13ft 4in and the height to top of cab is 8ft 7in. Allison semi-automatic transmission is fitted. The Dyson semi-trailer has detachable rear wheels, leaving a platform length of 26ft for 45-60ton loads. Atkinson and Dyson both co-operated with the operator Graham Adams of New Malden in the final specification.

Bottom left: A Silver Knight T 3266C model tractor, with the original view-line cab giving exceptional visability for the driver, is fitted with a Cummins 250 diesel engine and ZF gearbox. It is coupled to a 32ft York semi-trailer.

19

Austin

Austin has been producing commercial vehicles since 1909. Its first effort was a small delivery truck of only 15hp, obviously using the chassis and parts of the early Austin cars. In 1913 Austin aspired to a 2½ton vehicle, which employed several novel features including electric lighting and the rear-wheel drive transmitted by a cone clutch.

Austin kept to light vehicles under 2ton until, early in 1939, it produced a completely new range of vehicles similar to the Bedford range and with a cab and radiator not unlike that of its competitor. This range covered the capacity from one to five tons; smaller vehicles still used the car chassis and some of its body parts. The 5ton vehicle was produced during the war for the War Department.

In 1948 peace-time production recommenced with the 2ton and 5ton models. The Austin 25cwt three-way van was produced in 1950, when all the range could be powered by the Austin petrol engine or the Perkins diesel.

In 1952 Austin and Morris merged to form the British Motor Corporation. Some unification of the two ranges began and identical vehicles could be found with the badge of either Austin or Morris on their radiators. Several of the vehicles shown in the illustrations here could also be seen on the roads under the other name.

Austin-Morris later joined with Leyland to form the British Leyland Motor Corporation.

Left: The Austin A30 car chassis and body parts form this A30 van with a carrying capacity of 5cwt used by the publicity department of an air charter organisation. Similar van bodies but slightly larger were also made on the A40 car chassis.

Above: Another adaption from a non-commercial chassis - in this case an Austin taxi. In the 1950s several London-based newspapers were using these vehicles for their deliveries.

Centre right: In 1948 Morris introduced the J series vans and after the merger the range was taken up by Austin. This illustration shows the 1ton van popular with local traders. The range continued with minor modifications until the 1960s.

Bottom right: A typical 3ton van produced soon after the merger with Morris. This vehicle is actually owned by British Road Services and used under contract by Allen & Hanbury Ltd.

Above: A design evolved between British Motor Corporation and British Road Services for a 3ton parcels van. The chassis is modified with drivers foot controls moved back 11in and steering altered accordingly, which enable the driver to enter and leave his seat without clambering over the wheelarch. The body has 600cu ft capacity and a floor height of only 3ft 3in. The cab is fitted with sliding door and the driver can walk through to the rear. Known as 'Noddy Vans', many hundreds of this type were built in 1958-9.

Centre right: The Austin Champ was introduced as a competitor to the successful Landrover, but was never as popular. In 1962 softer springing was added as a refinement.

Bottom right: A 10ton articulated refrigerated vehicle with a 1,100cu ft Bonallack body. The refrigeration unit is driven by a Ruston and Hornsby diesel engine installed at the front of the trailer body.

Bedford

General Motors of America acquired the Luton firm of Vauxhall Motors at the end of the 1920s, and as they had been trying to expand the market for their Chevrolet range it was natural that production and design should at first be based on these models. The name changed to Bedford and they became the best-known light commercial vehicles produced during the 1930s.

During the war years the Bedford 15cwt and 3ton army lorries were known to British troops everywhere. In later years the range included the 3ton QL series of four-wheel drive vehicles.

In 1947 the Bedford range consisted of two light vans, a 5/6cwt and a 10/12cwt; a 30cwt truck; a 2/3ton truck (two wheelbases); a 3/4ton truck; and a 5ton truck. All these models were available with two differing wheelbase lengths. In addition there was a short-wheelbase 8ton tractor. All these models were of the normal control type and generally similar to the pre-war models.

The big 7ton models were introduced in 1950; these had semi-forward control with a completely redesigned cab. Various changes were made subsequently to the range,

Above: This 30cwt van of distinctive appearance was first produced in May 1946 and had been designed before the war, but production was held over until the cessation of hostilities. It had a six-cylinder petrol engine and a body of wood and metal construction. Overall length 16ft 4in, width 6ft 2in and height 6ft 8in.

including the fitting of a diesel engine in 1953. In 1955 it was claimed that more Bedfords were built — 64,773 — than any other British vehicle.

In 1960 the famous TK range, with the engine mounted transversly immediately behind the driver's cab, made its appearance. New 8cwt vans came on to the market in 1964, many of the components belonging to the Vauxhall Viva car chassis. The KM range, taking Bedford into the heavy market, appeared in 1966 with vehicles up to 24tons gross weight, a figure raised further in 1972 when 32ton tractor units were introduced.

A motto adopted by Bedford some years ago was "Bedford — You see them everywhere" — a statement that must be true even today.

BY APPOINTMENT
CABINET MAKERS

TO H.M. THE KING
& UPHOLSTERERS

C

WYLIE & LOCHHEAD.
LIMITED

HOUSE & SHIP FURNISHERS,

BUCHANAN STREET,

REMOVERS
STORERS
SHIPPERS

GLASGOW

TELEGRAMS
"WYLIE"
GLASGOW

Above: For the first few years after the war, the main
Bedford range differed little in outward appearance from
the pre-war models, as exemplified by this 2ton Luton-
type van purchased in 1949.

Top: After the war many wartime features and vehicles were released on to the civilian market. Bedford made a few military type models available and of course, many ex-Services vehicles were sold and 'civilianised'. This is a mobile display unit for use at agricultural shows, etc.

Above: In the early 1950s the range was redesigned, some models being known as the 'Big Bedfords'. This SB type tractor unit is coupled to a semi-trailer van incorporating a refrigeration unit. The van holds 95,000 ice-creams and is used for supplying outlying depots.

Right: The ubiquitous 15cwt van has proved popular for 20 years or more. Known as the CA van, it has a payload of 10/12cwt. It had the same four-cylinder 1594cc engine as used in the Wyvern car of that period. As can be seen it has semi-forward control and the overall length is 12ft 10in or 13ft 10in.

Below: Several transport operators, especially those engaged in household removals, use the Bedford passenger chassis with a van body. This one is on the Bedford S-type bus or coach chassis and has an unladen weight of 4tons.

REMOVALS STORAGE FULLER'S

REMOVALS STORAGE FULLER'S LONDON, S.E.17.

PHONE — ROD. 4346

196. WALWORTH RD LONDON. S.E.17

913 BMD

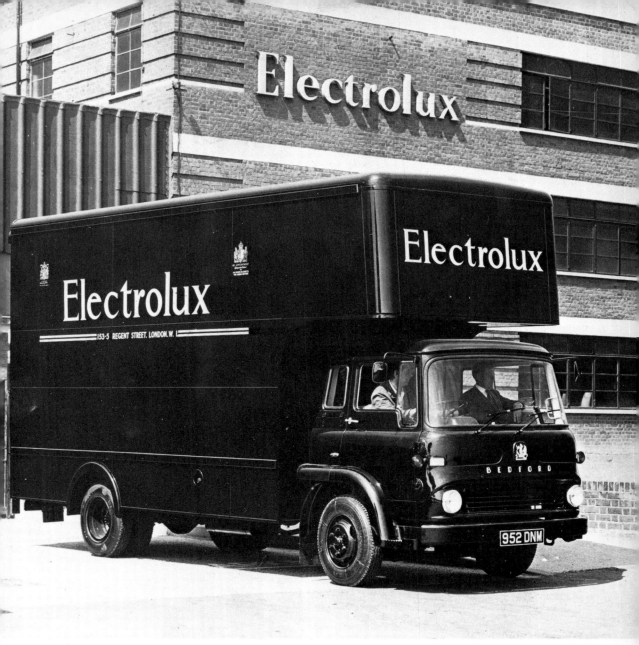

Top left: In the mid-1950s the A type was introduced. This was a normal control chassis which covered the range from 30cwt to 5ton with a variety of different wheelbase versions. It could be fitted with a petrol or diesel engine. The illustration shows a 5ton chassis with Mann Egerton box body for Special Pooled Deliveries.

Bottom left: This 10½ton lorry is a Primrose conversion made by lengthening the chassis and adding an additional axle. The overall length is 22ft 6in and the gross vehicle weight is 15ton.

Above: A complete redesign of engine and chassis effective over most of the Bedford range took place in the mid-1960s. The engine is mounted at the back of the cab and is accessible by gull wing lifting panels at the rear. This gives a roomy cab with exceptional good visibility, as shown with this 5ton van.

Bristol

The Bristol Tramways and Carriage Co was founded in 1906 to run motor buses in the Bristol area. It manufactured its first buses in 1908 and some were sold to outside operators. The company was acquired by the Tilling Group of bus operators, which in turn was nationalised in 1947, passing into the control of the British Transport Commission. As a result, Bristol only produced vehicles for nationalised bus companies.

In 1948 Bristol produced its first goods vehicle chassis for the Road Haulage Executive, later renamed British Road Services — the nationalised part of the road transport industry. This was a rigid eight-wheeler, with a maximum carrying capacity of 24tons gross weight (the limit at that time), powered by a Leyland 0600 diesel engine of 140bhp. A total of 500 was produced. Later the cab was redesigned and an articulated prime-mover introduced (model HA6G) with a Gardner 6LX diesel engine. The overall length of this unit was 34ft 6½in. Production ceased in 1965.

Bristol was de-nationalised and is now part of the Bus and Truck Division of British Leyland but no longer manufactures commercial vehicles, keeping to single and double-deck buses.

Below: The Bristol rigid 8 for a 15ton payload. The cabs are made of light alloy and fibreglass to save weight and the vehicle is fitted with a Leyland 600/2 diesel engine of 9.8litre.

Above: The type HA6G prime mover has a Gardner 6LX engine of 10.45litre. The semi-trailer gives the articulated unit a gross length of 34ft 6½in.

Below: A later version of the same unit showing redesigned cab for improved visibility.

BMC

BMC — the British Motor Corporation —
was formed following the merger of Austin
and Morris in 1952 and commenced to
integrate the two companies' designs to a
certain extent. In the latter part of the 1960s
vehicles began to appear with the BMC name
on their radiator grille. When the British
Motor Corporation was taken into the
Leyland empire in 1968 the practice
continued until 1970, whereafter the smaller
vehicles were marketed under the auspices of
Austin-Morris and the larger ones absorbed
into the Leyland Redline range.

Above and below: A close-up illustration of the
nameplate on the grille of one of the BMC Laird range
of vehicles and the lorry itself. It was available in
three rigid chassis forms, five wheelbase lengths and
fitted with 5.1 or 5.7litre diesel engine.

Left: The EA series of vans; this one, the 350EA, permits a 30cwt payload and has a walk through cab and underfloor engine. It is available in two body lengths offering 274cu ft or 322cu ft, with a choice of 70bhp petrol or 2.5litre 66bhp diesel engine.

Below: The Mastiff 16ton rigid four-wheeler powered by a Perkins V8 engine. A tilt cab is fitted. This vehicle is in the service of a Yorkshire textile concern.

Commer

Commercial Cars Ltd was founded in 1905 and the familiar name Commer became a contraction of the official title. Rootes Securities Ltd acquired control of the company in 1928. In the 1930s a range of light-to-medium weight vehicles was produced, extending from 10cwt vans to 5ton goods vehicles. During the Second World War, the Commer factories produced over 20,000 vehicles, including the tractor unit for the 60ft semi-trailers used by the RAF and known as a 'Queen Mary'.

After the war the range consisted of the Superpoise normal control vans and lorries ranging from 8cwt to 4/5ton vehicles, available in two wheelbases for tipping or haulage work. There was also a Commer-Hands 6-8ton tractor trailer unit, while the 25cwt van could also be obtained in a forward control version.

In 1948 Commer was quick to design a completely new range of 5 and 7ton vehicles with full width cab, full forward control and the engine mounted under the floor. These vehicles proved popular with many operators and were seen with a wide variety of bodywork.

A two-stroke diesel engine was marketed in 1953 having two horizontally opposed pistons in each of the three cylinders. The engine was fitted to certain of the range, but alternative Perkins diesels could also be fitted.

New Superpoise models were announced in 1955 for the 2-5ton range with a six-cylinder diesel engine, and the 15cwt and 25cwt vans had a four-cylinder engine.

A new range of forward control medium-weight vehicles appeared in 1963, later superseded by the V range. In 1966 heavy lorries of up to 16tons weight were produced.

One of the big design achievements of Commer vans was the 'Walk-thru van' introduced in 1961. With semi-forward control, the vehicles have been in production with only slight alterations for many years.

In 1970 the Rootes Group was acquired by Chrysler of America. Although production continued it was slowed down and at the time of writing the Commer vehicle is not the common sight it used to be on the roads of Britain.

Above: The Commer Superpoise range from 2ton to 5ton was announced in 1955. This 4ton van has a Perkins P6 diesel engine, but a petrol alternative was offered. It has a 13ft long body and is used for the transport of meat by the Peterborough & District Co-operative Society Ltd.

Peterborough Co-operative Service

298

COMMER

Above: This forward control 7ft 9in wheelbase tractive unit dates from 1955, for loads of up to 12ton. It is coupled to a 25ft long Hands semi-trailer with canopy top.

Centre right: A 7ton cattle truck with traditional bodywork. It is powered by a Rootes six-cylinder diesel engine, mounted under the floor of the cab.

Bottom right: In the small delivery van range this 15cwt Superpoise van was one of many supplied to the London *Evening News* in 1957.

36

Top: The Commer 'Walk-Thru' vans have been popular and 1½ton and 2½ton models are available. This 2½ton model has a special body for stacking provisions.

Above: In 1962 the Maxiload 12ton tractor was introduced. Fitted with a Rootes diesel engine, it is shown here coupled to a Taskers semi-trailer, the van body of which has a capacity of 1,134cu ft.

Dennis

Dennis Brothers Ltd produced its first commercial vehicle in 1904, and up to the outbreak of the Second World War in 1939 was turning out a range of medium and heavy vehicles as well as fire-appliances, in which it seemed to specialise.

During the war Dennis produced many vehicles for the services as well as a large number of trailer-pumps for use by the National Fire Service.

In 1948 the range consisted of the Pax 5ton, the Max 6-8ton and the new Jubilant 12ton six-wheel chassis, having a five-speed gearbox and a 5litre engine later enlarged to 5½ litres. This engine also powered the Centaur forward control 6-7ton lorry.

The Horla prime mover was introduced soon afterwards and this obviously had its origins in the pre-war models known as the 'Flying Pigs', because their bonnet protruded forward of the front axle; this remark also applies to the normal control Pax models.

In 1954 Dennis marketed an entirely new underfloor-engined van which they called the Stork. The engine was the horizontal version of the Perkins P4 and the van had a payload of 3tons. For loads of 24tons the Maxim was introduced in 1964. It was fitted with the then brand-new Perkins V8 diesel engine. In the late 1960s the whole range was redesigned as the Dominant, a 1ton lorry with a wheelbase of 14ft 5in, and the Defiant, a tractor with a wheelbase of 9ft 6in.

Throughout the period Dennis Bros has continued to specialise in fire-appliances, ambulances and refuse collectors. Examples of some of these are shown in the appropriate chapters.

Below: In 1946 the 'Flying Pig' was revived from the pre-war design. This 3½ cu yd end-tipping lorry was employed by the County Borough of Derby, one of many municipalities using the make.

Above: The Dennis Jubilant was introduced in 1946 as a rigid-6 12ton chassis powered by the Dennis six-cylinder diesel engine. A five-speed gearbox (including overdrive) and three differentials were fitted. The body length was 24ft.

Below: The forward-control Pax 6ton model was available with 70bhp side-valve petrol engine, an 80bhp overhead-valve petrol engine or with a Perkins P6 engine. Three wheelbase lengths were also available.

Above: This Dennis Maxim 28ton gvw prime mover has been popular with fleet operators. It is powered by a V8 diesel engine which is economical and reliable.

Right: A Pax V low-loading 16ton gross weight platform lorry. It has a wheelbase of 14ft 2in or 16ft 11in, the latter permitting a body space of up to 24ft. It is powered by a Perkins six-cylinder direct injection diesel engine.

Dodge

The American firm of Dodge Brothers founded an English subsidiary company in 1922 importing the 15cwt chassis direct from the parent concern. After four years small premises were acquired near Park Royal (London) and assembly of chassis from the imported components began as well as a certain amount of body-building. Dodge Bros was acquired by the Chrysler Corporation in 1929, although it continued to produce vehicles bearing that name. The English factory moved to the headquarters of Chrysler in the United Kingdom at Kew and settled down to produce an all-British vehicle under the Dodge label. In 1933 the first of these vehicles emerged on 30cwt and 2ton chassis, both using American engines and gearboxes. However, within a year 3, 4 and 5ton lorries were being produced. The semi-forward control, or short-bonneted 5ton chassis became a firm favourite for operators hauling sand and gravel and many were purchased prior to the Second World War.

After the war production continued at Kew and models from 2tons to 6tons were available with petrol or Perkins diesel engines as alternatives in the lower sizes. In 1954 the introduction of the Perkins R6 diesel engine enabled a 7ton truck to be made. These models were superseded by an entirely new range of normal control vehicles in 1956 and two years later by a forward control range, which over the years has extended to vehicles of up to 22ton gvw.

Dodge is now part of Chrysler United Kingdom Ltd and with Commer and Karrier forms the British truck division of that company. Dodge is now concentrating on vehicles in the 16-28ton range.

Below: This 5ton van shows its pre-war parentage, but was supplied in 1947 to F. R. Gerard for the transport of an ERA racing car, spares and equipment. It was chosen for its high cruising speeds.

Top left: The first post-war design is shown in this Model 123 6ton tipper. It had a petrol engine, but a diesel was later offered as an alternative. The wheelbase of the tipping chassis was 9ft 11in. Two other wheelbase lengths were also available for lorry or van bodies.

Bottom left: In the 1960s this form of cab was introduced and in outward appearance was similar to those fitted to some of the Leyland range. This 8ton chassis carries a 1,750gal milk tanker, which could be vacuum loaded at a rate of 100gal per minute.

Top: The K type forward control model supplied in 1968 to the Esso Petroleum Co Ltd to carry a 2,800gal tank for bulk fuel distribution.

Above: This is a Dodge KT900 six-wheel tipper with a wheelbase of 14ft 1in fitted with a Perkins V8 diesel engine. The vehicle has a plated gvw range up to 24ton. The KT900 is fitted with tandem drive and two-speed rear axle, and five-speed gearbox.

ERF

ERF are the initials of Edwin Richard Foden, a member of the illustrious family who broke away from the parent organisation in 1933 to produce diesel-engined vehicles on his own account. Coventional design, reliability and long service gained the make the respect of the transport industry before the outbreak of the 1939 hostilities. The range of 6-15ton models continued after the War, but first the radiator grille was extended and later the V-type driving cab with a 'wrap-round' windscreen was introduced in 1949. This was followed by other cab designs and one which had an oval radiator grille. Up to this time it was usual for a Gardner engine to be fitted, but models with AEC and Rolls-Royce engines were offered as alternatives and the American Cummins engine was also available from 1962.

The company has concentrated on the heavy haulage side of the market and always kept ahead of the latest developments. Power-assisted steering was introduced in 1958, then reinforced plastic cabs as an alternative to all-steel were made available and the new A-type cab appeared in 1971. The ERF tractive units have become a familiar sight on the Continent, where they haul the large inter-Continental trailers from the UK to European countries.

Below: A 7½ton ERF lorry of traditional design, the front end being similar to that of all vehicles manufactured between 1946-53.

Above: An 8-wheeled 4,000gal tanker powered by a Gardner 6LW oil engine, with a five-speed gearbox and a double-drive bogie with third differential. The vehicle was supplied new in 1958.

Below: A new design of cab and radiator introduced from the early 1960s, seen here on an articulated unit for 30ton gtw. The tractor is a 64GX model with Gardner 6LX engine, a David Brown six-speed gearbox with overdrive and a Kirkstall double-reduction bevel rear axle. The semi-trailer is a Hands 24½ton tandem axle type. Running fully laden the fuel consumption averages 10mpg.

Above: The B series in service in 1975. A type 31G4 in 1975 operated by a Lincolnshire operator for the bulk transport of grain. The tipping body is 26ft long and has a 36cu yd capacity. The B series low-profile cab has the external cab panels fitted to a safety cage framework.

Right: In 1973 this ERF Type MCC 340 Cummins-powered 32ton GCW tractor was being used on a weekly express service from Stoke-on-Trent to Basle in Switzerland. The Continental type all-steel sleeper cab gives drivers maximum comfort and the vehicle is fitted with twin 50gal fuel tanks and automatic lubrication.

Foden

Edwin Foden, founder of the present firm, perfected a compound steam traction engine in 1880. He experimented with many steam wagons until, in 1900, success was achieved with an overtype boiler vehicle having a payload of 3tons. This was the forerunner of a long and successful line of steam vehicles, which were produced until 1931.

The decision to commence manufacture of diesel-engined lorries was probably made around 1929, although the first vehicle did not appear until two years later. It began Foden's long association with Norris Henty and Gardner Ltd. Gardner engines are still used in Foden vehicles, although alternatives are now offered.

In the eight years up to the outbreak of the Second World War a large number of commercial vehicles was produced, ranging from 4ton to 15ton capacity; all had the distinctive Foden cab and radiator, which was still retained after hostilities had ceased. During the war production was centred on 6 × 4 Army lorries with spherical cabs (first produced in 1936), also Centaur and Crusader tanks as well as munitions of various types.

In 1946 an order was received from the Steel Company of Wales for a large-capacity tip lorry and the first of many giant dump trucks was manufactured. This particular one looks quite small compared with the huge vehicles now built. In the same year the revolutionary Foden two-stroke diesel engine was produced.

Air brakes and power-assisted steering were introduced in 1956. The Commercial Motor Show press notices acclaimed this as the 'pacemaker for the next five years', but two years later a new department at the Sandbach works produced the reinforced plastic cab, making Fodens the forerunner in this particular field as well. Four years later the cab was again modified to tilt forward and given complete and unobstructed access to the engine and mechanical components.

The present range of Foden vehicles is extensive and all models still retain a distinctive appearance.

Below: A 7½ton standard lorry fitted with a Gardner 6LW oil engine as marketed in 1949.

Top left: The FE4/8 8ton lorry was introduced in 1954 and fitted with a new engine — the Foden FD4, a four-cylinder version of the famous Foden two-stroke engine. It developed 84bhp at 2,000rpm. An 18ft light alloy platform body is fitted to the vehicle shown.

Centre left: The famous FG range replaced the DG models in the early 1950s. It is exemplified by this FG6/15 chassis powered by a six-cylinder Gardner engine and fitted with a 12-speed gearbox. The special body is capable of carrying 300 sheep in one load.

Below: A Gardner 6LX diesel engine powers this 32ton gross weight articulated unit with a Yorkshire Tri-axle 33ft-long semi-trailer.

Above: A 28ton rigid-8 for carrying steel girders up to 51ft in length. The low-height cab seats four and permits the girders to be carried over the roof. The operator believes that this 35ft-long vehicle has advantages over an articulated one. Similar low-height cabs have been used for mobile cranes.

Below: The 1970s version of the Foden 4× 2 tractor, showing the S60 all-steel cab with a back-sloping windscreen. Another version of the cab — the S70 — has the same outline but is constructed from reinforced plastics, while there is a half-cab variation known as the S50. Turbo-charged Cummins engines are the ususal power units.

Ford

The American firm of Ford was a pioneer in mass production and commenced to export parts of its cars and light vehicles to the UK in 1904. Seven years later an assembly plant at Trafford Park began the construction of the famous model T, using more and more parts produced in this country. In 1915 a model T 7cwt van appeared and this chassis was used for a variety of different bodies, the chassis being extended and strengthened for leads up to 1ton. The model A was produced in 1928 and in 1931, the whole plant was moved to Dagenham, where the production was entirely British.

There can be no greater comparison of progress than the early model T and the latest H models now being produced.

During the war the UK branch of the Ford Motor Co produced the six-wheel winch lorries for the balloon barrage, Bren and Universal tracked and half-tracked carriers, and a vast number of general service lorries, including the four-wheel drive forward control 3tonners. In 1948 the range of vehicles was from 5cwt to 5ton, including the Surrey and Sussex six-wheelers, although these were soon withdrawn. The trade name Thames was adopted and the diesel engine offered as an alternative on the larger-capacity vehicles, the 4D and 6D originally being V8 petrol-engined models. The Thames was superseded by the Thames Trader and the D1000 range was introduced for gross weights of 28tons.

While Ford was producing vehicles in the UK the later years' designs, such as the highly successful Transit vans, have shown their American parentage. There is also close co-ordination between Dagenham and the German factories.

Below: The Ford Thames 15cwt van, popular with the small retailer in the late 1950s and early 1960s, was the forerunner of the highly successful Transit van.

Above: A demonstration of how to drink beer can't be a bad thing! A 2ton Ford Thames van, to which a four-cylinder petrol or diesel engine could be fitted. A 3ton van had similar dimensions, but was fitted with larger tyres and servo-assisted brakes.

Below: In the early 1960s Ford introduced the K500 series of Thames Trader truck with normal control layout, but with alternative petrol or diesel engines. It was available in several differing wheelbases and had a load capacity of up to 8ton. This version is a 7ton truck with a wheelbase of 15ft 4½in.

Top: This semi-forward control Ford Thames Trader is fitted with a Ford 4D diesel engine. The vehicle has a length of 22ft and a 12ft 8in wheelbase for the carriage of 5ton loads, but alternative wheelbase versions were available, also tractive units for semi-trailers.

Above: A Ford D800 pantechnicon showing how the floor of the Luton head of the body is hinged to allow the cab to tilt forward and give access to the engine and mechanical components. The Ford D series catered for loads from 4ton to 8ton, and included a short wheelbase tractor for use with semi-trailers. The series was introduced to the market in the mid-1960s.

Above: A Ford DT2417 model 6 × 4 22ton gvw tipper with 12ft 3in wheelbase shows the articulation and springing of the road wheels.

Below: In 1974/5 Ford introduced its largest commercial vehicle, the H series. This Irish registered articulated unit makes weekly trips between Ireland and Holland via England.

Guy

The first Guy commercial vehicle was a
30cwt lorry produced in 1914. It was fitted
with a direct drive in third gear for use when
fully laden; when travelling light, an
indirect top gear was used. This idea years
later was looked upon as something original
and called an 'overdrive'. Vehicle production
forged ahead with several innovations, like
an articulated vehicle produced as early as
1922. In 1933 the Wolf 2-tonner was
introduced, quickly followed by the Vixen 3-
4ton chassis and the 6ton Otter. Production
of these vehicles, said to be ahead of their
time, was continued until 1938, when the
Government requested the company to
produce military vehicles; this it did in large
quantities until 1945, when civilian
manufacture was recommenced, using the
pre-war designs with improvements. Except
for minor changes, the designs remained
basically the same until 1952, when a new
all-steel cab was designed for the Otter. In
the following year a short-wheelbase Otter
model was made available as a tractive unit
for use with semi-trailers.

To cater for the heavier market, the Big
Otter was produced in 1954 for loads of up to
8tons and the Invincible range of four-, six-
and eight-wheelers for up to 12, 20 and 24tons
gross respectively, which were the maximum
legal loads permitted in the UK at that time.
These vehicles were available in several
chassis lengths and with a choice of engines.
Two years later the Warrior models were
introduced for 14ton payloads; they had a
similar cab style to that of the Invincible
model.

In 1961 the company was taken over by
Jaguar Cars Ltd. In 1964 a range of vehicles
to a brand-new design, known as the Big J
series, was put on to the market; at the time
of writing this is still in current production.

Throughout its existence Guy Motors has
always been in the passenger vehicle field.
Thus when taken over by Leyland Motors, it
was transferred to the jurisdiction of
Leyland's Bus and Truck Division. But alas,
the famed Red Indian and the motto 'Feathers
in our Cap' is no longer seen proudly adorning
the radiator caps of Guy vehicles.

Above: During the war, Guy Motors were allowed to
manufacture a few vehicles for delivery to operators
on priority work. This Vix-Ant 4ton lorry is an
example; it has the same bonnet and radiator styling
as the Army vehicles.

Top left: A post-war Vixen 4ton van. A four-cylinder 3,686cc petrol engine was fitted.

Bottom left: The Invincible range of heavy-duty vehicles was introduced in 1954. This 15ton chassis has a tank body for an operator specialising in the transport of bulk liquids.

Above: With a gross train weight of 15ton, this Warrior articulated tractor, powered by a Gardner 4LW oil engine with a five-speed gearbox and two-speed rear axle, is coupled to a Scammell semi-trailer.

Centre right: The Warrior range was produced in 1958 and was available with a variety of engines. This 6ton van has the same cab style as the 12ton and 15ton models. There was also a tractor for articulated vehicles.

Bottom right: A Guy Big J 16ton gwv of 1968 with a 2,500gal tanker. An AEC AV505 engine is fitted.

Jensen

In 1939 Jensen Motors of West Bromwich and the Reynolds Tube Co designed some special lightweight vehicles which at that time were powered by Ford four-cylinder petrol engines. It was a chassis-less design and the use of aluminum and light alloys kept the unladen weight of the vehicle to under 3tons. At that time the law stated if a vehicle weighed under 3tons unladen it could travel at more than the 20mph limit then in force for heavy vehicles and still carry a 6ton payload. These early Jensen vehicles used parts of the Ford 3ton range.

A fresh approach to the problem was made in 1946, when the first Jensen lightweight commercial vehicles were put on the market. They were especially designed for the carriage of bulk capacity loads. The integral construction of the main frame and the superstructure as one unit in special light alloys allowed the vehicle to have a platform length of 23ft, or a pantechnicon body of up to 1,632cu ft could be mounted.

Perkins P6 six-cylinder 70bhp oil engines were fitted. The engine complete with radiator, clutch and gearbox could be withdrawn in 30min, a replacement engine and units reconnected and the vehicle be ready for the road in another two hours. The wheelbase was 16ft 2in and the overall length 27ft 6in.

Left: A 6ton lorry again powered by a Perkins P6 diesel engine. This engine is easily withdrawn by removing the distinctive JNSN radiator grille and pulling the engine forwards.

Below: A Jensen lightweight van powered by a Perkins P6 engine and designed for the transport of bulky loads. Aluminium alloy has been used extensively for the body which is integral with the chassis.

In 1951 Jensen Motors introduced a four-wheeled articulated tractor and trailer which they called the 'Jen-Tug'. This used an Austin engine of the same type as in the Austin A40 Somerset saloon cars. It was not very popular and few Jen-Tugs were produced.

Production of Jensen Commercial Vehicles ceased in 1956. The raising of speed limits and other legislation made the lightweight vehicle unnecessary; furthermore the cost of repairs to these vehicles was very high even in those days.

Karrier

Karrier vehicles were originally manufactured by Clayton & Co of Huddersfield, who produced a small 30cwt lorry in 1908. It was followed by heavier vehicles including 3,000 lorries for World War I. In 1920 the name Karrier Motors was registered and production progressed in medium and heavy vehicles, while in 1931 the Karrier Cob mechanical horse or three-wheeled tractor was introduced.

The Rootes Group took control of Karrier Motors in 1934 and manufacture was transferred to the Commer factory at Luton, where the Bantam was produced. During the war, Karrier made many vehicles for the Army including armoured cars. When peacetime production was resumed the Bantam range was continued, albeit redesigned in 1948/9, and the CK3 vehicles in the 3-4ton range were introduced. These were superseded by the Gamecock model with underfloor engines and similar in design to the Commer range — in fact in 1963 the Gamecock was fitted with a new design of cab identical to those on Commer vehicles.

In July 1970 the control of Karrier passed to Chrysler United Kingdom Limited. It would appear that since then some Commer vehicles have been sold with the Karrier nameplate and vice-versa.

Below: The Bantam was introduced before the war and continued in production virtually unaltered during the 1950s. It was popular because of its low loading height (around 2ft 6in from the ground), as displayed by this 30cwt van, used for the collection and delivery of refrigerators in the retail ice-cream trade.

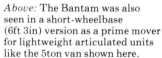

Above: The Bantam was also seen in a short-wheelbase (6ft 3in) version as a prime mover for lightweight articulated units like the 5ton van shown here.

Centre left: In 1948/9 the CK3 model was produced. It was a 3/4ton lorry, and the forerunner of the Gamecock introduced in 1952.

Bottom left: In 1952 the successful Bantam was provided with a redesigned front end as far as the bodywork was concerned. This mobile shop is typical of many built on the 2ton chassis.

61

Landrover

The Rover Company produced its first car in 1904 but had never entered the commercial vehicle field. During the Second World War it was manufacturing many vehicles for the War Department. Afterwards, in 1949, the British Army sought a vehicle similar to the American Jeep, which had been so successful in numerous wartime campaigns and served in many countries with the British and American troops.

So it was that in 1949 the first Landrover four-wheel drive vehicle with a 7ft 4in wheelbase (11ft 1in length) made its appearance. It was powered by a 1,600cc engine and had a payload of 15cwt. In 1952 a longer wheelbase (9ft 1in) version was introduced and a 2litre engine could be offered as an alternative. In 1957 a 2litre Rover diesel engine could also be fitted.

These Landrovers have been supplied for various bodies, including trucks, hard-tops, caravans, estate vehicles, fire appliances etc. A forward control version is also available.

In 1970 the Range-Rover was introduced, again with four-wheel drive (permanently engaged) and powered by a 1,130bhp V8 petrol engine. This is extensively used by police forces in the UK for accident and traffic control work, where its high speed proves an advantage.

The Rover Company became part of the British Leyland empire in 1967. More Landrovers have been built and exported than any other light four-wheel drive vehicle in the World. By August 1974 over 900,000 had been produced.

Above: This is the long wheelbase Landrover, having an overall length of 14ft 7in and 9ft 1in between the axles. The regular wheelbase is 7ft 4in with a body length of 11ft 10in. The Landrover is also available as a forward control vehicle, but is shown here as a small fire appliance with HCB Angus firefighting equipment.

Left: The larger and more luxurious Range Rover was introduced in 1970 and has permanent four-wheel drive. The wheelbase is 8ft 4in and the overall length of 14ft 8in. This vehicle has a special body for police work and is used by many forces for motorway patrols.

Leyland

The name Leyland Motors Ltd was adopted in 1907, but before that the firm was producing steam wagons under the name Lancashire Steam Motor Co, which produced its first petrol-engined lorry in 1904. Leyland has been responsible for many developments in the commercial field. Backed by a brilliant team of engineers, such as Sir Henry Spurrier, it has gained a great reputation for reliability and good design over the years.

It could be said that the 3ton vehicles built during the 1914-18 war under a subsidy scheme — the RAF Leyland — helped to make the company's name in the transport world. Between the wars the firm was producing large numbers of heavy haulage vehicles for a wide variety of loads. Its 1939-45 wartime production record was an impressive one; the firm was building five different types of tank, including the Cromwell and Comet, as well as supplying vehicles and other munitions to the Fighting Services.

One of the first post-war ranges of goods vehicles was the very successful Comet semi-forward control 5-7ton models distinguished by their new frontal styling. In addition, Leyland was expanding and developing its normal range of vehicles.

In 1951 the old-established Scottish firm of Albion Motors was acquired and in 1955 Scammell Lorries of Watford. In 1962 Leyland took over AEC, which had already absorbed Maudslay, Crossley, and Thornycroft; thus the Leyland Motor Corporation became one of the largest commercial vehicle-producing plants in the World. At the 1964 Commercial Vehicle Show a new range of trucks was announced for loads from 16tons to 32tons, all of which featured the new Ergonomic cab designed primarily for driver comfort, plus the fact that it could be tilted forward to give instant access to the engine.

During 1968 the British Motor Corporation (formed from the merger of Austin and Morris) also joined the Leyland empire; thus the medium range of vehicles it produced also came under the Leyland banner. The following years saw some form of standardisation. In 1970 the goods vehicle range was again extended with the introduction of the Bear 20ton six-wheeler, followed in 1972 by the new Buffalo range of models up to 32tons, but all using the same cab and other components.

Leyland has made many conquests in the export markets of the world, and continues to do so.

Left: The Leyland Comet model was a post-war vehicle of distinctive appearance. With semi-forward control, it had a Leyland six-cylinder diesel engine. A five-speed gearbox and an Eaton two-speed axle. Two wheelbases were available for lorries and vans, one for tippers and one for tractive units. This illustration shows one of 150 used for cement deliveries by Associated British Portland Cement.

Above: A Leyland Octopus of 1956 provided with the new cab style introduced the previous year, at the same time as air brakes and the 150bhp 11.1litre diesel engine. This version has a Bonallack light-alloy box body, for carrying up to 12ton of bacon.

Right: The Super Comet 90 forward control model was introduced in 1954. This illustration shows a pantechnicon type body which is 30ft long by 8ft wide.

Left: Following the merger of Austin and Morris in the Leyland empire, the medium-weight vehicles were completely redesigned. This photograph shows the Redline 4 × 2 lorry which was available with a choice of engine sizes for payloads from 3½ton to 11ton. The range was built at the Scottish plant of Leyland.

Below: Another vehicle in the medium capacity range was the Terrier for gross vehicle weights of 6½, 7½, 8½ and 9½ton. A choice of engines was available, but all models had syncromesh gears, power-assisted hydraulic brakes and 16in or 20in wheels. The cab is the same design as that used on the Boxer range for 1970.

Top right: This Leyland Beaver model carries the same name as pre-war models, but that is the only similarity. A six-cylinder diesel engine provides 240bhp for this 9ft 6in wheelbase tractive unit with a gross carrying weight of 32ton.

Bottom right: A 1970s version of the Leyland Octopus to contrast with the illustration of the 1956 version. This tanker operates at 26tons gross carrying weight with 2,000gal of sulphuric acid.

Maudslay

Maudslay was an established manufacturer of marine and other steam engines when it produced its first motor lorry in 1905. Production of commercial vehicles continued thereafter and several outstanding models were created in the 1920s and 1930s.

The range introduced immediately after the war was actually to have been shown at the Commercial Motor Show in 1939, but this was cancelled due to the outbreak of war. It consisted of the Mogul, a 6ton four-wheeler; the Militant, a 7cu yd tipper; the Mustang, a 10ton six-wheeler; the Maharajah, a 13ton six-wheeler; the Maharanee, a 13ton tractor; and the Meritor, a 15ton eight-wheeler.

The Maudslay Motor Co was acquired by AEC in 1948 and for a few years afterwards produced vehicles to its new owner's specification and with the AEC badge. Production ceased in 1954.

Below: The Mogul, the smallest vehicle produced by Maudslay, was a two-axle 7½ton payload lorry with a wheelbase of 13ft 6in for the Mk II version or 16ft for the Mk III.

Above: This Mustang double-front axle six-wheeled van can carry a payload of 10ton and has a body length of 20ft. It is powered by the AEC 7.7litre CI engine.

Left: The largest vehicle in the Maudslay range was the 29ft 11½in long Meritor rigid eight-wheeler to carry a payload of 14-15ton. This vehicle is shown being loaded with corrugated iron sheeting at London's Royal Albert Docks.

69

Morris Commercial

Prior to 1924 Morris had merely produced light vans and trucks on its motor car chassis, using common components. However, the introduction of the 1ton chassis gave them an entrée into the commercial market and the range was slowly extended. From 1948 vehicles for a larger load capacity were introduced, including a new range of forward control lorries, although normal control models were kept in production up to 5tons capacity for some years. Several alternative engines were offered including a 100hp six-cylinder engine, and the 5ton payload-and-upwards vehicles could use the new diesel engine manufactured in association with Saurer.

In 1952 Morris merged with Austin to form the British Motor Corporation and gradually some standardisation took place between the two makes. In 1959 the FG series of forward control models was introduced, but finally the merger of British Motor Corporation and Leyland meant that all models were issued under the BMC or Leyland marque.

Below: Still produced up to 1953, the Morris 5cwt van based on the series E Morris Car. This illustration is a 1948 version, but it remained basically the same until replaced by the chassis and components of the Morris Minor car.

Left: This six-cylinder 5ton lorry was introduced in 1948, although the development had started in 1937. It had several new features, not the least interesting being the diesel engine which had been designed from the earlier Saurer engines. The new-style driving cab and radiator were quickly used on other models in the Morris range.

Below: A 1946 production 25/30cwt van of the LC series, featuring a four-cylinder 15.9hp petrol engine, a body capacity of 245cu ft and a 9ft 9in wheelbase. A 15/20cwt forward control van was also introduced to a similar design.

Left: The FG series was introduced in the early 1960s and featured cab doors inclined to the rear, to enable the driver and passenger to alight (or enter) without the risk of obstructing traffic. The body shown in this illustration carries a 2ton payload of frozen foods.

Right: The Morris LD series of 1ton and 1½ton vans as illustrated here was a pooled design with Austin introduced in 1954. Although the vehicles were marketed with different names on the bonnet, they were identical except that generally the Austin version had four slits in the radiator grille. The vehicles proved popular with local authorities and police forces as well as with the retail and distributive trades.

Below: This 5ton normal control, petrol-engined lorry was similar to the design of the heavier pre-war Morris vehicles. It was a striking design and in someways ahead of its competitors. The all-steel cab would seat three persons.

Scammell

Scammell Lorries Ltd was established in 1922 following some experiments with articulated vehicles and the obvious advantages to be gained from this form of lorry. In addition, the firm produced a frameless tanker and a rigid-6 lorry. It concentrated on vehicles for the heavy haulage section of the road transport industry and its tractive units, all of which were fitted with chain drive to the rear wheels, soon became famous. A rigid eight-wheeler was also produced in the mid-1930s.

There was a deviation from the heavy haulage market in 1933, when the first Scammell mechanical horse was produced for 3ton and 6ton loads. With its facility for quick coupling to semi-trailers, it soon proved very popular and manufacture has continued to this day.

During the war Scammell produced a large number of tractors for artillery use, as motive power units for tank transporters and recovery vehicles. Many of these were purchased by civilian organisations from Government sales and saw service for more than 20 years with public works contractors, transport recovery firms and fairground operators.

In the early 1950s the range consisted of the 15ton rigid-8, the Mountaineer 4 × 4 as a rigid or prime-mover; and the Constructor, a 6 × 6 load carrier or prime mover fitted with a Rolls-Royce engine. This range was increased with newer models such as the Handyman 4 × 2 tractor and the Routeman rigid 8, both available with alternative choice of engines and wheelbase lengths.

Scammell Lorries Ltd were acquired by the Leyland organisation in 1955.

The 1974 range of large tractors for heavy haulage was the Contractor, Samson and Super Constructor. The range of tractive units for semi-trailers was the Crusader, Handyman, and Trunker.

In addition several varieties of large dump trucks are manufactured, many for export, also specialised vehicles for oil-field works.

Left: A typical Scammell rigid eight-wheeler for 15ton payload equipped with Gardner or Meadows six-cylinder diesel engine and a six-speed gearbox. The full forward control position allows a bodyspace 24ft 6in in length.

Above: The normal control tractor proved popular with many hauliers for widely different loads. It is available with the same engines and gearbox as the rigid 8 and is coupled to a two-axle semi-trailer, having a payload capacity of 15ton. It is shown here coupled to a 3,300gal tank.

Right: The latest version of the three-wheeled mechanical horse was called the Scarab. Powered by 25bhp or 45bhp petrol engines mounted behind the cab, the tractor is coupled to a semi-trailer having a capacity of 3ton or 6ton. The version shown here is in the service of British Rail.

Above: The Highwayman tractor unit produced in the early 1960s was for 30ton loads and was a development of the standard tractor. Note the modern look given to the sloping bonnet and the deep front wings with built-in headlamps.

Centre left: The Routeman II rigid 8 fitted with six-cylinder Leyland or Gardner engines. The overall length was 29ft 9in and the 30cu yd tipping body for the haulage of grain shown here was built of light alloys.

Bottom left: The Trunker II twin-steer motive power unit for operation at 32ton gcw. The front axle of the pair at the rear is fitted with single tyres and turns like the front axle.

Top right: The Contractor high-speed heavy haulage prime mover can be fitted with Leyland, Rolls-Royce, Cummings or other special engines to customers' requirements. Usually fitted with eight forward and two reverse gears, it is designed for up to 240ton gcw.

Bottom right: The Crusader articulated tractor for 32 ton gcw, normally fitted with 220bhp or 280bhp Rolls-Royce diesel engines. It is shown here operated by a soft drinks firm for trunk haulage.

Seddon

Foster and Seddon had been engaged in the commercial vehicle industry as repairers and distributors for 18 years before it entered the manufacturing side in 1937. Its first vehicle was a forward control lightweight 6ton chassis fitted with a Perkins P6 engine. This proved popular with many varied operators. After the war production recommenced and was increased with an expanding range.

In the 1960s the emphasis was more on the heavy models. These were often equipped with Gardner engines and included a 16ton gcw four-wheeler which can also be used with a draw-bar trailer.

In 1970 Seddon Motors acquired control of Atkinson and became known as Seddon-Atkinson Vehicles Ltd.

The International Harvester Corporation of America took control of Seddon Atkinson in 1974, having already gained a foothold in Europe through its acquisition of the Dutch DAF concern.

Below: The post-war 6ton chassis differed little from its pre-war counterpart, as this Perkins diesel engine version for a Yorkshire brewery shows.

Top right: The first change from normal Seddon production was the 3ton range which appeared in 1952. It was available on normal, tipper or tractor wheelbases and is shown here coupled to a mobile office for the Automobile Association with an unladen weight of 6ton 9cwt. Sleeping accommodation for a crew of two is provided.

Bottom right: The 25 diesel delivery van made its appearance in 1954 for a payload of 25cwt. The engine, the P3, was the smallest in the Perkins range. The van shown here was one of three in experimental service with the General Post Office.

Top left: An attractive radiator grille forming part of the body on this 6/7ton van used by a Nottingham firm of removal specialists.

Bottom left: Seddon finally branched out into the heavier field and this vehicle was delivered in 1963. It is a 24ton eight-wheeled chassis carrying a 4,000gal tank and powered by a Gardner 6LX engine.

Top right: A four-wheel tractor similar to the 13/4 models of 1966, this is powered by a Perkins V8 engine and is intended to haul a gross combined weight of 26ton.

Centre right: A 13/4 platform lorry powered by a Perkins four-cylinder fuel injection engine having a wheelbase of 16ft 9in. Two other wheelbase lengths are available for tractor or tipper operation. The vehicle has a gross weight of 17ton.

Below: A 13/4 tipper having a wheelbase of 14ft 8in. The 600cu ft double-skinned alloy tipping body carries bulk loads of grain or animal foodstuffs.

Sentinel

The history of Sentinel begin with Alley and McLellan, who as general engineers, experimented with road vehicles and in 1906 produced a steam-propelled prototype. In 1918 the works was moved to Shrewsbury and the Sentinel Company as we know it today was inaugurated. The firm made its name with steam wagons which were highly successful in four-, six- and eight-wheeled versions, the latter carrying a payload of 14tons. The models manufactured prior to the war all had modern equipment, including electric speedometers, lights, power take-off, and self-stoking arrangements for the boiler.

In the period reviewed in this book the firm concentrated on goods vehicles and some bus chassis. The commercial models were in the medium range of 6-10tons on four- and six-wheel chassis, all having a Sentinel diesel engine mounted horizontally on a frame behind the cab, which was of standardised design incorporating sliding doors on all later models.

The firm ceased production in 1957 and the Shrewsbury works was taken over by Rolls-Royce.

Below: Ancient and Modern. A 1954 photograph showing a 1927 Sentinel steam wagon working alongside a recently delivered vehicle in South Africa.

Above: Fitted with a Sentinel-Ricardo horizontal diesel engine, this 7/8ton lorry is also used to tow a four-wheeled trailer.

Left: A re-designed front grille was fitted to many Sentinel lorries in 1952. This view shows the unobstructed cab and ease of entry.

Shelvoke and Drewry

Shelvoke and Drewry has been a specialised manufacturer since inception in 1923. Its first models were small-wheeled, solid-tyred vehicles with tiller steering and a transverse engine situated under the driving seat. All models were forward control. Their low platform height and easy manoeuvrability — once the driver had mastered the tiller steering — made them popular with municipalities for refuse collection and light low-loading work. Some SD chassis were also used for small buses.

Nowadays the firm produces a more conventional vehicle for refuse collection work. It is powered by a Leyland or Perkins engine, but Shelvoke and Drewry manufactures its own chassis and bodywork with a fibre glass cab, some of which accommodate a crew of four in addition to the driver. Many of the bodies feature the Pakamatic or Revopak refuse-collecting bodies. With a capacity of 40 or 50 cu. yds, very much more hygenic and clean than the old side-loaders which were the norm in pre-war days.

Left and below: In 1950 this fore-and-aft tipper was popular.

NEW 353

Thornycroft

One of the few names which pioneered motor transport still with us is Thornycroft. Although it is now part of the Special Products Division of British Leyland, the first Thornycroft steam wagon was on the road in 1897 and the firm had an impressive record of production until it was taken over by AEC Ltd in 1961 and subsequently merged with British Leyland.

Apart from vehicles for general goods haulage, Thornycroft often manufactured specialised chassis for overseas requirements. Such models as the Antar were typical of this field of operation.

In 1948 the production range was the Nippy 3ton, Sturdy 5/6ton, Sturdy 8ton tractive unit and the Amazon 12ton six-wheeler. In 1958 the Mastiff 7ton chassis was introduced and in 1960 a new and attractive cab which had pronounced rounded front panels, including the glazing, was applied to all models. Just over a year later production of normal chassis virtually stopped. Now the name is confined to specialised vehicles for airport fire-fighting and oilfield work.

Below left: A Trusty maximum-load rigid eight-wheeler with all-metal cab and 24ft platform body operated by the Angus Milling Co Ltd of Kirriemuir, Co Angus.

Right: A Sturdy Star 5ton platform lorry. Light alloy construction of cab and bodywork enabled the unladen weight to be kept within 3ton. A normal control version of this model used the cab components from the bonneted Trident range.

Below: A Swiftsure 6ton box van with the 1959 version of the Thornycroft cab and radiator grille. The Bonallack built body is 16ft long.

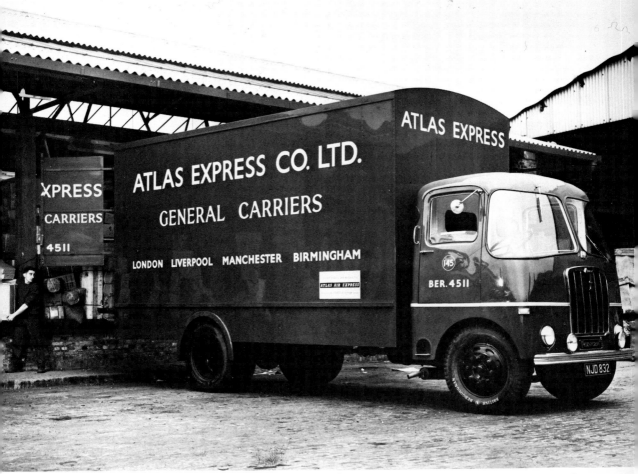

Above: The redesigned front end of the Trusty eight-wheeler of 1959. The Thompson-built 4,000gal tank body has six compartments for the transport of fuel oil.

Top right: A comparison for size! A Thorncroft Antar tractor alongside a Morris 1000 saloon. The Antar has a turbo-charged Rolls-Royce diesel engine and a Self Changing Gear Co semi-automatic eight-speed gearbox.

Right: An Antar six-wheel tractor unit as used by many heavy haulage specialists for large indivisible loads. It is capable of gross train weights in excess of 100ton. One is shown here coupled to a Crane trailer moving a 100ton stator for Uskmouth power station.

Trojan

Trojan was always a subsidiary of the Leyland Company. Its first model was produced in 1924 to provide work for Leyland employees, and to utilise spare machinery to manufacture a small and economical vehicle. The latter had solid tyres a four-cylinder two-stroke engine developing 10hp and chain drive. The commercial van was for 5cwt loads and was used extensively by Brooke Bond Tea Co. In 1928 work was transferred from Kingston to Croydon and the company set out on its own with a smaller production, but nevertheless produced 7cwt and 10cwt models to the same basic design. The range

Above: A Trojan 1ton delivery van powered by a Perkins P3 diesel engine. These vehicles proved very economical during the fuel shortage following the Suez crisis when motor fuel was rationed.

continued thus until the war, plus a small number of six-wheeled vehicles.

In the late 1940s a completely new design was produced with a payload of 15-20cwt using a Trojan 65 four-cylinder two-stroke engine or a Perkins P3 three-cylinder diesel. A short wheelbase tractor was also produced using the same motive power and components, including the cab pressings.

The last Trojan design emerged in 1958, when a 25cwt forward control model was announced again utilising the Perkins P3 diesel engine. This model was also used as a mini-bus and possibly more of these were produced than the commercial vehicles.

The company ceased operations in the early 1960s.

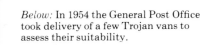

Below: In 1954 the General Post Office took delivery of a few Trojan vans to assess their suitability.

Above: A Vulcan 6VF model, which was the standard vehicle with the exception of the special livestock container body built by J. H. Jennings of Sandbach, Cheshire. The vehicle had a wheelbase of 13ft.

Right: Another standard Vulcan used for the delivery of beer. It was a 6ton vehicle fitted with a Perkins P6 diesel engine.

Vulcan

Vulcan is only just eligible for entry into this book. Although formed in 1903 to produce commercial vehicles and buses, the firm merged with Tilling-Stevens — a famous name in road transport — in the late 1930s. Production was transferred to the latter company's works at Maidstone in Kent and was taken over by the Rootes Group in 1953. This Group already owned Commer and Karrier and thus the Vulcan make was absorbed into the existing companies and the name Vulcan disappeared.

The Vulcan range consisted of a 6ton forward control lorry with a Perkins P6 diesel engine and a short wheelbase tractor for semi-trailer work, using the same components and engine.

Fire Appliances

The design of fire appliances, like other forms of transport, has changed over the years. No longer do firemen have to stand on the 'footboards' holding on to the ladders; they now sit in comparative comfort in totally-enclosed, limousine-type coachwork. The clanging bell has been replaced by the twin-tone horn and the traditional red livery has in some areas been replaced by panels of polished aluminum or even yellow paintwork.

Up to the 1950s the chief manufacturers were Dennis and Leyland, later joined by AEC. In the 1970s the popular makes seem to be Dennis and ERF, although several municipalities and County Councils have favoured vehicles on some of the lighter chassis by manufacturers such as Ford.

The term fire appliance — it should never be called a fire-engine — is used here in the general sense and envelops the many differing types of vehicle such as pump escapes, turntable ladders, emergency tenders, hose-laying lorries and salvage corp tenders. In addition there are specialised vehicles for airport and airfield services etc. Space allows only a few vehicles of the last 30 years to be included in this chapter.

Below: A development of the standard pump escape unit as used by the London Fire Brigade, this version was introduced in 1955. It has a Dennis F101 chassis and a Rolls-Royce 12litre diesel engine. The pump is capable of delivering 1,000gal of water per min. The gross weight of the vehicle is approximately 9ton.

Above: A Commer 5ton chassis fitted with underfloor-mounted petrol engine forms the basis of this appliance used by the Kent Fire Brigade. The Hampshire Car Body coachwork has sides of unpainted embossed aluminium. The vehicle carries 3,000ft of hose and has a 30/35ft extending ladder.

Below: A Merryweather turntable ladder mounted on an AEC chassis in the service of the London Fire Brigade. The special cab gives complete protection to the crew when travelling.

Top: Leyland ceased production of fire appliances for a time at the beginning of 1940. This Leyland Firemaster is the second of the new range when production was resumed in 1960. It is operated by the City of Glasgow Fire Service and is powered by a 150hp Leyland diesel engine mounted amidships under the floor. The bodywork is by David Haydon Ltd of Birmingham.

Above: A Bedford TK series 7½ ton chassis forms the basis of this turntable ladder used by the City of Birmingham Fire Service. The Magirus 100ft turntable ladder is hydraulically-operated and the body, built by David Haydon Ltd, has a specially-designed cab to give a low overall height to the vehicle of under 10ft.

Above: A water tender for the Norfolk Fire Brigade has a Ford Type D1014 chassis and ERF bodywork. It is similar in design to other appliances on the Ford chassis used by many municipalities and borough councils.

Below: An ERF Firefighter water tender powered by a Cummins V8 diesel engine through an Allison fully automatic transmission. The Waterous pump can deliver 1,000gal per min at 200lb sq in pressure.

Having devoted a short chapter to Fire Appliances, it is only right that a selection of ambulances and refuse collection vehicles etc be shown. Again, changes have obviously been made to the available chassis on the market in the 30 year period covered by this volume. Bodywork has kept pace with the modern developments and plastics now play an important part in the interior fittings for ambulances.

Below: A Spurling de-luxe ambulance body on a Bedford chassis as used by Vauxhall Motors in 1947.

Above: A Wadham's body made of polyester resins reinforced with fibre glass fitted on a Morris LD2 chassis with Dunlop Pneuride air suspension and supplied to Salop County Council in 1960.

Left: The standard-type ambulance adopted in 1964 by the London County Council, which collaborated in the design. The body is fitted to a modified BMC model LD chassis.

Top right: A 1974 Dormobile 'National Ambulance' body on an extended (12ft 2in) wheelbase Bedford CF chassis with General Motors automatic transmission. The vehicle shown is one of many for the London Ambulance Service.

Bottom right: A Wadham GRP ambulance body on a Ford Transit 150 chassis powered by the Ford V6 2.5litre petrol engine with automatic transmission.

Top: A typical example of early post-war refuse collector. This side-loading Dennis vehicle has a capacity of 10cu yd and was supplied to the County Borough of Chesterfield.

Above: A Dennis Paxit II model of an end-loading, compression-type refuse collector with six-man cab supplied to the Borough of Sutton and Cheam in 1960. The number plate does not denote maximum speed!

Above: An 800gal gully emptier on a Thornycroft Sturdy 13ft 4in wheelbase, petrol-engined chassis. The vehicle employs an Eagle tank and hydraulically-operated end-tipping gear. Supplied to Sutton-in-Ashfield Urban District Council.

Centre left: A Karrier-Yorkshire 750gal gully emptier powered by a Perkins P6 engine. The vehicle was introduced to prospective purchasers in 1954.

Bottom left: A Karrier road sweeper of 1950 which retained several of the features of the pre-war models, such as the curved road brush, patent elevator gear and water sprinkler. This model has servo-assisted brush lifting gear, and a hydraulic end-tipping body of 2ton capacity. It is powered by a six-cylinder engine of 80bhp.

Breakdown Vehicles

From the earliest days of motor transport there has always been the possibility of a breakdown, to say nothing of an accident, thus there has been the need for a breakdown vehicle, whether it be for a simple towing operation or a recovery from a difficult situation.

In pre-war days a simple rear mounted crane, often on an old lorry chassis would suffice, but such equipment even with up-to-date motive power is now confined to the towing of cars or small vans.

It was not so long ago that the only really heavy recovery vehicles belonged to the fire brigades of the larger towns and cities, some of the larger passenger transport undertakings, or one or two specialised hauliers such as Pickfords.

After the war many garages set up as so-called recovery specialists often operating with ex-WD vehicles having improvised home-made equipment. There was also the birth of the 'accident pirates', small firms and individuals who positioned their vehicles at strategic places close to the main arterial road and listened to the short wave radio used by the Police, so they often arrived at the scene of an accident before the more essential services. These 'pirates' usually operated with an ex-WD Jeep, Landrover or Austin Gipsy.

As legislation allowed goods vehicles to become larger and carry heavier loads, so the breakdown vehicle had to increase in size and capacity, so that nowadays it has become a specialised vehicle operated by a specially trained crew. Such vehicles are usually fitted with four-wheel drive, large power operated winches, twin boom cranes which have been developed from an American idea, heavy-duty hydraulic jacks, oxy-acetylene cutting apparatus, and a host of other equipment. A recent innovation is a large inflatable air-cushion to absorb the impact and minimise further damage when righting an overturned vehicle.

Right: Typical of many heavy breakdown vehicles, a converted Army lorry. In this case it is an American Diamond T which had been the motive power unit for a tank transporter.

Top: A specially-built recovery vehicle. The chassis is the AEC Mammoth Major six-wheeler powered by the AV 691 diesel engine. The vehicle is capable of towing 56ton loads and the bodywork and fittings were constructed by the operator, C.V. (Sales & Repairs) Ltd at Basildon. The cab has been modified to give a workshop area at the rear with full-height standing room. Mounted on the back is a Dial-Holmes twin-boom wrecker. Equipment includes twin fog lamps, with floodlamps on each boom.

Above: A purpose-built ERF vehicle for their firm's own service centre. Powered by a Cummins six-cylinder diesel engine, the drive is through a 15-speed gearbox. The ERF Type MW all-metal cab will seat five. The heavy-duty 20ton crane was supplied by TFL Cranes, which also provided other recovery and towing equipment carried on this vehicle.

Above: Based on a Ford 28ton drawbar tractive unit this recovery vehicle has a Holmes twin-boom crane and two power winches, each capable of 12ton capacity. The vehicle, which cost £8,000 in 1965, is powered by a Ford 511 V8 diesel engine and operated by Invicta Motors of Canterbury, Kent.

Centre left: A new Foden eight-wheeled recovery vehicle, fitted with a Dial-Holmes twin-boom crane, stands beside a 1954 breakdown truck which was replaced in 1975. The operator is F. Crosse & Sons of Doncaster.

Bottom left: For the small or light recovery jobs the ubiquitous Landrover is ideal and the four-wheel drive facility is greatly appreciated when towing heavy dead weights. This vehicle is typical of its type and operated by Mann Egerton.

Fairground Vehicles

The inclusion of this chapter may seem a strange choice, but road transport is the life-blood of the travelling showman. This is where many vehicles end their days, long after their contempories have left the normal general-haulage field.

Many ingenious and well-thought-out modifications are often made by the showmen to adapt a vehicle to suit their particular requirements. The work is usually undertaken by the amusement caterers themselves, demonstrating how competent many of them are as mechanical engineers. Especially popular with many showmen is the diesel-powered prime mover which does not carry a load, except a diesel generating set, but can haul up to three large trailers, each carrying a maximum load. This is exactly what the large steam road- locomotive (showmans' traction engines) undertook before the diesel engine took over in the late 1930s.

A large 'Dodgem' machine usually needs at least two 8-wheeled lorries each pulling a massive trailer, plus a prime mover (with generating equipment) also pulling two trailers — the pay box and the owner's living-wagon. Semi-trailers or articulated vehicles are not usually found on the fairgrounds, because of the difficulty of manoeuvring them especially over rough terrain. Of recent years, however, there have been exceptions as some of the modern amusements are built-up using the semi-trailer as the basis (or platform) of the ride.

Current legislation has made it necessary — and prudent — for the showman to have more up-to-date vehicles, thus many fairly modern 8-wheelers can be seen carrying the special bodies taken off older lorries. (All photographs by the author.)

Bottom left: George Pickard ran this 1914 Tilling Stevens petrol-electric vehicle until the early 1970s. It is believed the chassis was part of a Brighton bus withdrawn in 1925, and afterwards converted to pneumatic tyres. The Tilling Stevens vehicles were popular with showmen as they had a ready-made generator for their own power supplies.

Right: A veteran Leyland c1929 seen at Harewood House Steam Fair and Rally in August 1970.

Below: A few vehicles have been specially built for showmen and this Foden was commissioned in 1938 by W. Nichols of Banbury. It is fitted with a Gardner 6LW diesel engine and will take a 50ton payload. The vehicle was still in use in June 1977.

Top: The Scammell Showtrac was designed especially for travelling showmen in 1946. The 20ton chassis is fitted with a 100bhp diesel engine, and the integral body contains another diesel engine for generating up to 450 amps, a winch and a ballast block for adhesion. Many vehicles like this now carry the nameplate taken from the owner's original steam road-locomotive sometimes after a period of 35 years or more.

Above: The use of ex-War Department vehicles proved a reliable and economic source of transport for many amusement caterers after the war. This ex-Army Scammell tank-transporter with a body built by the new owners is typical of many which were to be seen on the fairgrounds in the 1960s and early 1970s.

Above: The ex-WD AEC Matador 4 × 4 heavy artillery or gun-tractor was another vehicle which proved extremely popular with showmen throughout the country.

Below: This ex-WD Albion artillery-tractor was used by W. Irving and Sons until 1975 to haul part of their Gallopers load.

Top: This Albion box-van seen here at Mitcham in 1972 commenced life with a haulage contractor in 1935 and is a credit to its owners — past and present.

Above: A Thornycroft Amazon delivered new to Whiteleggs Amusements in February 1948, and named 'Vanguard' after the firm's steam road-locomotive. It carries two generating sets but the original 100bhp diesel engine has been replaced by a Gardner 6LW. This was one of three machines supplied to the firm and the last in service before it was withdrawn and scrapped in the early 1970s.